yum
crocl

12 projects too cute to eat!

D0380007

KRISTEN RASK

STERLING INNOVATION
New York

contents

Part One: Fruits & Veggies

Part Two: Main Dishes

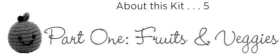

Part Three: Desserts

Introduction

Hello! Hopefully, if you have either bought this kit or received it as a gift, it means you are interested in the world of "amigurumi." Amigurumi has become very popular over the past six years with an increasing collection of pattern books, patterns sold on Etsy, and a cult-like following amongst collectors. If you have never been exposed to this sort of art, amigurumi is the Japanese word for knitted or crocheted stuffed animals and other creatures.

What makes these adorable creatures so appealing? Most of these patterns are simple pieces easily made in a few short hours. They often have a lot of personality and are both appealing to adults and kids.

Over the past few years, food items have become popular as new crocheted friends. For this kit, I'm happy to share some of my favorite designers and their unique creations with you. These projects are quite easy, and you will become a pro in no time. And soon, you'll be creating your own designs!

Happy crocheting!

—Kristen Rask

crochet hook
Metric Conversion Chart

US	Metric (mm)
B/1	2.25
C/2	2.75
D/3	3.25
E/4	3.50
F/5	3.75
G/6	4.00
7	4.50
H/8	5.00
I/9	5.50
J/10	6.00
K/10.5	6.50
L/11	8.00
M/13	9.00
N/15	10.0

About this Kit

COMPONENTS:

This kit comes with everything you need to make two patterns in this book, a chocolate cupcake and a chocolate donut with white frosting. Included are the following components: a crochet hook, fiberfill for stuffing, a metal yarn needle, four black safety beads (for eyes), brown yarn, pink yarn, white yarn, and black thread.

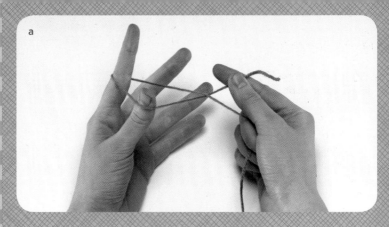

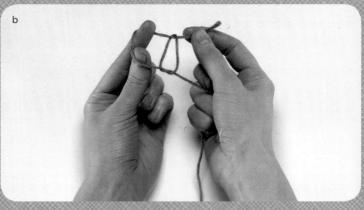

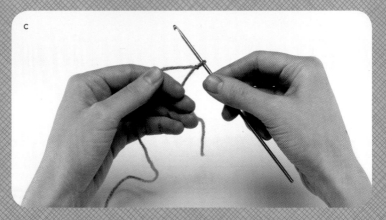

TECHNIQUES AND TERMINOLOGY:

Before you start any of the twelve cute patterns in this kit, practice the various stitches and learn their abbreviations.

Slip Knot: Every crochet project begins with a slip knot.
1. Wrap the yarn around your finger, creating a loop with a 6" tail. (see fig. a)
2. Pull one end of the yarn through the loop to create a knot. The knot should be taut, but not too tight to slip your hook through. (see fig. b and c)

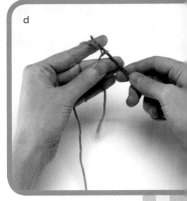

Yarn Over (yo): A basic technique that's used frequently, "yarn over" simply means to wrap the yarn over the hook.
1. With your hook in your right hand and your yarn in your left, pull the yarn around from behind the hook.
2. The strand of your "working yarn" (the yarn coming from the skein) should be across the throat of your hook on top.

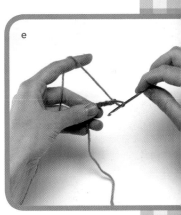

Slip Stitch (sl st): This stitch is used to connect pieces, strengthen edges, or fasten off stitches.
1. Insert hook into stitch.
2. Yo and pull through loop.

Chain Stitch (ch): The foundation of any project, the chain stitch is either worked in rows or in a ring. For most of the projects in this book, you will be working in a ring.
1. To begin a chain stitch, start with a slip knot. (see fig. d)
2. Yo, then draw yarn through the loop, making the first stitch. Continue working in this manner until you have desired amount of stitches. (see fig. e)

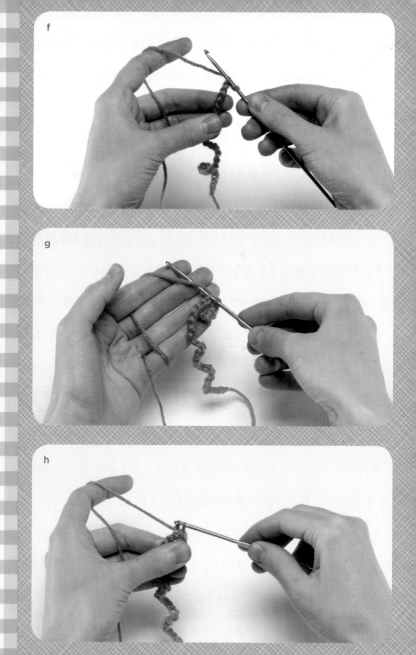

Working into the chain: Occasionally a pattern will say to work into the front or back of a chain. The front of the chain looks like a series of V's, and the back of the chain has a ridge (or bump) behind each chain stitch.

Single Crochet (sc):

1. Insert hook into desired stitch.
2. Yo and draw yarn through loop. You will now have two loops on your hook. (see fig. f)
3. Yo again and draw yarn through both loops to complete a single crochet. (see figs. g, h, and i)

Adjustable Ring: Because amigurumi pieces are made mostly "in the round," the adjustable ring is the first step of many patterns and is an invaluable technique to master. An adjustable ring is used to mark where the circle begins and ends, so you can keep track of which row you're working on.

1. Chain two times (ch 2).
2. Sl st through the first stitch. Each pattern will then tell how many single crochets to make in the ring.

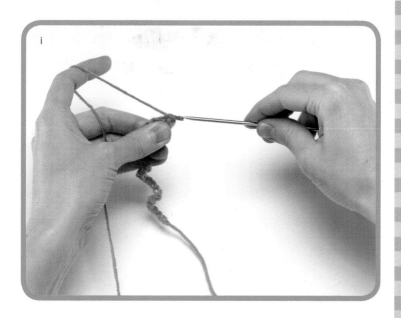

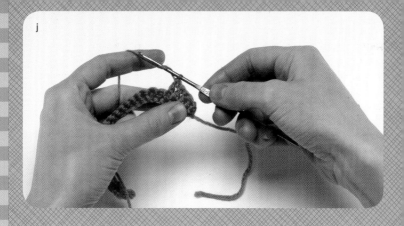

j

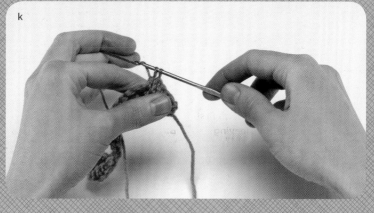

k

l

Half Double Crochet (hdc): This stitch is between single crochet and double crochet in height.
1. Yo and insert the hook into the desired stitch.
2. Yo and draw yarn through the stitch, leaving three loops on your hook.
3. Yo one last time and draw yarn through all three loops.

Double Crochet (dc): The double crochet, the most commonly used stitch, is taller than the single crochet.
1. Yo first, then insert hook into a desired stitch. (see fig. j)
2. Yo, then draw your hook through the stitch, leaving three loops on the hook. (see fig. k)
3. Yo, then draw yarn through first two loops on the hook, leaving both loops on hook.
4. Yo one more time and pull yarn through last two remaining loops. (see fig. l)

Treble Crochet (tr): This stitch is used to make the longest stitches.
1. Yo two times, then insert hook into desired stitch.
2. Yo and draw yarn through stitch, leaving you with four loops on the hook.
3. Yo and draw yarn through the first two loops, leaving three loops on the hook.
4. Yo again, and draw yarn through the last two loops, leaving just one loop.

Decreasing (sc2tog): This abbreviation for decreasing means to single crochet the next two stitches together. By doing this, you will combine stitches, making the piece smaller.
1. Insert hook into desired stitch.
2. Next, insert hook into the next stitch after that, leaving three loops on the hook. (see fig. m)
3. Yo, then draw yarn through all three loops. (see figs. n and o)

Front Post Double Crochet (fpdc): Yarn over, insert hook from the front of the post, going into the back, then coming out to the front again, draw up a loop, yarn over, pull through 2 loops, yarn over, and pull through both loops.

Back Post Double Crochet (bpdc): Yarn over, insert hook from the back of the post, going into the front, then coming out to the back again, draw up a loop, yarn over and pull through 2 loops, yarn over and pull through both loops.

Adding yarn: To change colors or start on a new skein after running out of yarn, follow these simple steps.
At the end of a row:
1. Make a slip knot with the new skein, leaving a tail.
2. Insert the hook where you are to start crocheting.
3. Continue to follow pattern.

In the middle of a row, change yarn when there are two loops left on your hook:

1. Grab old yarn together with a six-inch tail of new yarn.
2. Yo the new yarn as usual.
3. Pull through the two loops on the hook, completing the stitch.

Weave in ends: This finishing step means to sew (or "weave") yarn into a finished piece to prevent unraveling. After cutting a 6" tail, thread yarn onto a yarn needle and weave through the back of the project's stitches. Do not go in and out of the project as it will appear on the finished side and show.

Hook size: At the beginning of each pattern, a desired hook size is listed. Hook sizes range from small at the beginning of the alphabet (nothing in this book is smaller than a C/2, the size of the hook included in this kit) to larger as the letters go on. The hook size affects the gauge, the number of stitches in a square inch, and will determine the finished project size. Tighter stitches will ensure that stuffing won't emerge through gaps, although they should be loose enough to work through them with the hook.

Reading a pattern:
The patterns in this book are mostly in rounds (Rnd), mean-ing instead of being made in flat "rows" of stitches, they're worked in circular rows of stitches, or "rounds." Some crochet makers use a stitch marker to keep track of the start of each round.

Asterisks surrounding instructions indicate to repeat that set of steps. A number within parentheses following asterisked instructions indicates how many stitches should be in that round, which can be highly beneficial to those new to crochet.

Example: *1sc, sc2tog, 1sc* (12) Translation: Single crochet in the first stitch, decrease the next stitch, and then single crochet again. Repeat this process until the round is finished, giving you 12 stitches in that round.

Parentheses inside asterisks are separate steps that need to be repeated in addition to repeating the entire asterisked set. In this book, an "x" should be read as "times." Example: *2sc in next stitch, (1sc) 4x* (12)

Translation: Single crochet twice in the next stitch, then single crochet into the next 4 stitches, and repeat.

Fruits & Veggies

corn on the cob

BY ANNA MOSCIONI FROM OHIO

- -

Oh, corn on the cob, you truly are one of the best parts of the summer! It is just so satisfying to shuck corn, and with this project, you can do it without all the mess. Designed by Anna Moscioni, this little vegetable is the perfect playful decoration for your kitchen. Just remember—you can't put this one on the grill!

what you'll need:

- C crochet hook
- baby yarn in Bright Green and Yellow
- pair of black safety eyes
- black yarn
- yarn needle
- stuffing

FINISHED SIZE: Approx. 7.5" tall

Instructions

CORN: Yellow and Bright Green
• Make adjustable ring in bright green.
Rnd 1: 6sc in ring (6)
Rnd 2: 2sc in each stitch (12)
Rnd 3: working in back loops only, 1sc in each stitch (12) **(see fig. 1a)**
Rnds 4–5: 1sc in each stitch (12)
• Switch to yellow yarn
Rnd 6: 1sc in each stitch (12)
Rnd 7: *1sc, 2sc in next st* (18)
Rnds 8–9: 1sc in each stitch (18)
Rnd 10: *(1sc) 2x, 2sc in next st* (24)
Rnds 11–30: 1sc in each stitch (24)
Rnd 31: *(1sc) 2x, sc2tog* (18)
Rnd 32: 1sc in each stitch (18)
• Attach safety eyes and sew on mouth. (see fig. 1b)
Rnd 33: *1sc, sc2tog* (12)
• Add stuffing.
Rnd 34: *(1sc) 2x, sc2tog* (9)
Rnd 35: *(1sc), sc2tog* (6)
• Close with sl st. Join a 12" length of white yarn to one of the stitches in Rnd 35.
• Weave tail through remaining 6sc and pull up firmly to close the hole. Secure end and trim so that it is approx. 3" long. Fray it out to resemble corn silk "hair." **(see fig. 1c)**

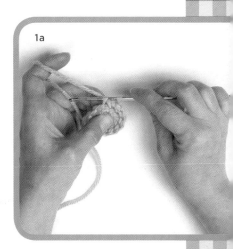

1a

HUSK: Bright Green
• Ch 18 and sl st to first ch to form a loop
Rnd 1: 1sc in each stitch (18)
Rnd 2: *(1sc) 2x, 2sc in next st* (24)
Rnds 3–4: 1sc in each stitch (24)
Rnd 5: *(1sc) 3x, 2sc in next st* (30)
Rnds 6–10: 1sc in each stitch (30)

- Work in rows to form the leaves.

Row 1: ch 1, turn, sc in next 15sc, ch 1, turn (15)

Row 2: 1sc in each stitch, ch 1, turn (15)

Row 3: sc2tog, sc in next 13sc, ch 1, turn (14)

Rows 4–5: 1sc in each stitch, ch 1, turn (14)

Row 6: sc2tog, sc in next 10sc, sc2tog, ch 1, turn (12)

Rows 7–8: 1sc in each stitch, ch 1, turn (12)

Row 9: sc2tog, sc in next 8sc, sc2tog, ch 1, turn (10)

Row 10: 1sc in each stitch, ch 1, turn (10)

Row 11: sc2tog, sc in next 6sc, sc2tog, ch 1, turn (8)

Rows 12–13: 1sc in each stitch, ch 1, turn (8)

Row 14: sc2tog, sc in next 4sc, sc2tog, ch 1, turn (6)

Rows 15-16: 1sc in each stitch, ch 1, turn (6)

Row 17: sc2tog, sc in next 2sc, sc2tog, ch 1, turn (4)

Row 18: 1sc in each stitch, ch 1, turn (4)

Row 19: (sc2tog) 2x (2)

Row 20: sc2tog (1)

- Finish off.
- Join green yarn on Rnd 10 at base of leaf you just made and repeat Rows 1-20 **(see fig. 1d)** above to make another leaf. Do not finish off. Continue to sc evenly around both leaves. Finish off and weave in ends. **(see fig. 1e)**

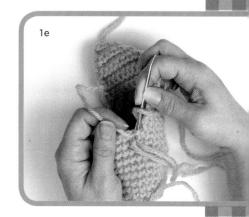

1e

oranges

BY DENISE FERGUSON FROM PENNSYLVANIA

Orange-you glad you are going to make this? Denise Ferguson has created the cutest oranges to add that much needed citrus to your crafting diet. This is a great project for play or an adorable decoration in your kitchen. Something both kids and adults can love!

what you'll need:

- C/2 crochet hook
- worsted weight yarn in Chocolate Brown, Bright Lime Green, Orange Popsicle, and Jet Black
- 3 pairs of black safety eyes
- yarn needle
- stuffing

FINISHED SIZE: Approx. 2.5" high

Instructions

STEM: Chocolate Brown
• Ch 3, 1sc in second ch from hook and next ch.
  Finish off, leaving long tail for sewing. (see fig. 2a)

LEAF: Bright Lime Green
• Ch 4, 1sc in second ch from hook, 1hdc, 1sc. Finish off, leaving long
  tail for sewing. (see fig. 2b)

ORANGE: Orange Popsicle, make 3
• Make adjustable ring.
Rnd 1: 6sc in ring (6)
Rnd 2: 2sc in each stitch (12)
Rnd 3: *1sc, 2sc in next st* (18) (see fig. 2c)
Rnd 4: *(1sc) 2x, 2sc in next st* (24)
Rnd 5: *(1sc) 3x, 2sc in next st* (30)
Rnd 6–10: 1sc in each stitch (30)
• Sew on leaf and stem, attach safety eyes, and sew on mouth. (see
  fig. 2d)
Rnd 11: *(1sc) 3x, sc2tog* (24)
Rnd 12: *(1sc) 2x, sc2tog* (18)
Rnd 13: *1sc, sc2tog* (12)
• Add stuffing.
Rnd 14: (sc2tog) 6x (6)
• Close with sl st, leaving
  tail for sewing. (see
  figs. 2e and 2f)

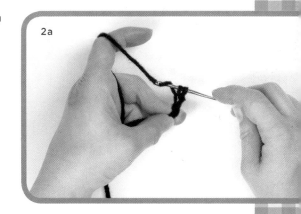

2a

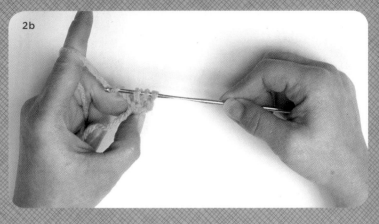

2b

2c

2d

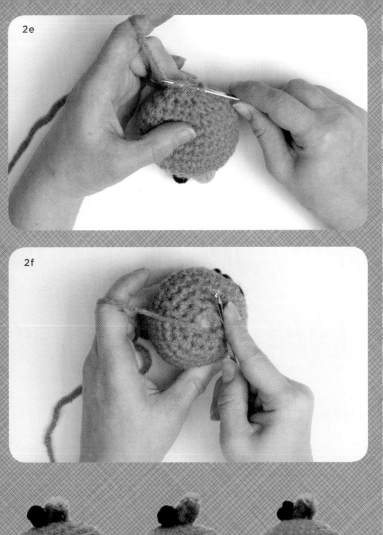

2e

2f

peas in a pod

BY TRISTINE BENEDICT FROM MARYLAND

Need a present for someone special? This little pea pod
makes a great gift for an anniversary or your best friend.
Because what's better for the one you love than two peas
in a pea pod? Designer Tristine Benedict tests all her latest
creations on her two kids. These are both adult and kid
approved!

what you'll need:

- G/6 crochet hook
- acrylic yarn in Fern
- 2 pairs of black safety eyes
- stuffing
- yarn needle
- sewing needle
- green thread

FINISHED SIZE: Approx. 2.5" long

Instructions

POD: Fern

Rnd 1: Ch 18, sc in 2nd ch from hook, 1sc in each st; working
on opposite side of foundation chain, 1sc in each st (34) **(see fig. 3a)**

Rnd 2: 1sc in each st (34)

Rnd 3: 1sc in each st (34)

Rnd 4: 1sc in each st (34)

Rnd 5: 1sc in each st (34)

Rnd 6: 1sc in each st (34)

Rnd 7: 1sc in each st (34)

Rnd 8: 1sc in each st (34)

• Close with sl st.

• Using needle and green thread, pinch end of pod and
  sew together 2 sts. Repeat on opposite end. **(see fig. 3b)**

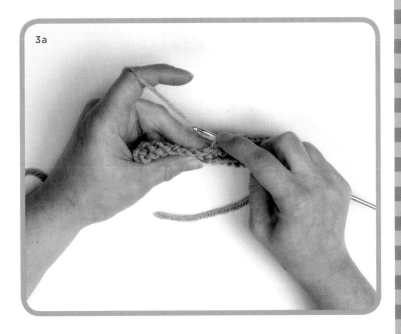

3a

3b

3c

3d

PEAS: Fern, make 2
• Make adjustable ring.
Rnd 1: 6sc in ring (6)
Rnd 2: 2sc in each stitch (12)
Rnd 3: *1sc, 2sc in next st* 6x (18)
Rnd 4: 1sc in each st (18)
Rnd 5: 1sc in each st (18)
Rnd 6: *(1sc) 2x, sc2tog* (12)
• Attach safety eyes between
  Rnds 3-4 and sew on
  mouth over Rnd 5 **(see fig. 3c)**
Rnd 7: (sc2tog) 6x (6)
• Close with sl st stuff, sew up open-
  ing, and weave in end. **(see figs. 3d
  and 3e)**

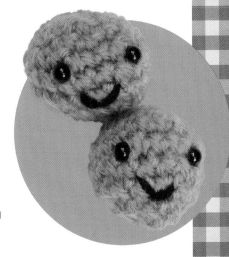

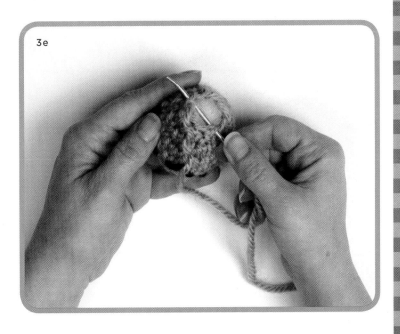

3e

turnip

BY ANNA MOSCIONI FROM OHIO

Turnips might not be the go-to vegetable at your house, but they will be once you start having these guys around! Who knew turnips could be so cute and cuddly? Made to perfection by Anna Moscioni, these root veggies are easy to make and appreciate. Make a whole bunch in no time!

what you'll need:

- E/4 crochet hook
- worsted weight acrylic yarn in Off-white, Light Purple, Dark Purple and Green
- pair of black safety eyes
- black yarn
- sewing needle
- stuffing

FINISHED SIZE: Approx. 9" tall

Instructions

TURNIP: Off-white, Light Purple, and Dark Purple
• Make adjustable ring.
Rnd 1: 6sc in ring (6)
Rnd 2: 1sc in each stitch (6)
Rnd 3: *1sc, 2sc in next st* (9)
Rnd 4: 1sc in each stitch (9)
• Pull the tail through the center of Rnd 1 to the outside
  of the turnip. These will be the roots.
Rnd 5: *(1sc) 2x, 2sc in next st* (12)
Rnd 6: *1sc, 2sc in next st* (18)
Rnd 7: *(1sc) 2x, 2sc in next st* (24)
Rnd 8: *(1sc) 3x, 2sc in next st* (30)
Rnd 9: *(1sc) 4x, 2sc in next st* (36)
Rnd 10: *(1sc) 3x, 2sc in next st* (42)
Rnds 11–14: 1sc in each stitch (42)
Rnd 15: Switch to light purple yarn and (1sc) 4x, switch
to off-white yarn and (1sc) 37x, switch to light purple
yarn and 1sc (42) **(see figs. 4a and 4b)**
Rnd 16: (1sc) 5x, switch to off-white yarn and (1sc) 33x,
switch to light purple yarn and (1sc) 4x (42)
Rnd 17: (1sc) 7x, switch to off-white yarn and (1sc)
5x, switch to light purple yarn and (1sc) 4x,
switch to off-white yarn and (1sc) 21x, switch
to light purple yarn and (1sc) 5x (42)
Rnd 18: (1sc) 8x, switch to off-white yarn
and (1sc) 3x, switch to light purple yarn
and (1sc) 7x, switch to off-white yarn and
(1sc) 3x, switch to light purple yarn and
(1sc) 3x, switch to off-white yarn and (1sc)
5x, switch to light purple yarn and (1sc)
4x, switch to off-white yarn and (1sc) 3x,
switch to light purple yarn and (1sc) 6x (42)

Rnd 19: (1sc) 25x, switch to off-white yarn and (1sc) 3x, switch to light purple yarn and (1sc) 6x, switch to off-white yarn and (1sc) 2x, switch to light purple yarn and (1sc) 6x (42)

Rnd 20: *(1sc) 5x, sc2tog* (36)

Rnd 21: switch to dark purple yarn and (1sc) 5x, switch to light purple yarn and (1sc) 30x, switch to dark purple yarn and 1sc (36)

• Attach safety eyes and sew on mouth.

Rnd 22: (1sc) 4x, sc2tog, 1sc, switch to light purple yarn and (1sc) 3x, sc2tog, (1sc) 4x, sc2tog, switch to dark purple yarn and (1sc) 3x, switch to light purple yarn and 1sc, sc2tog, (1sc) 4x, sc2tog, (1sc) 3x, switch to dark purple yarn and 1sc, sc2tog (30)

Rnd 23: (1sc) 3x, sc2tog, (1sc) 2x, switch to light purple yarn 1sc, sc2tog, (1sc) 2x, switch to dark purple yarn and 1sc, sc2tog, (1sc) 3x, sc2tog, switch to light purple yarn and (1sc) 3x, sc2tog, switch to dark purple yarn and (1sc) 3x, sc2tog (24)

Rnd 24: *(1sc) 2x, sc2tog* 2x, switch to light purple yarn and (1sc) 2x, switch to dark purple yarn and sc2tog, (1sc) 2x, sc2tog, 1sc, switch to light purple yarn and (1sc) 2x, switch to dark purple yarn and sc2tog, (1sc) 2x, sc2tog (18)

• Add stuffing.

Rnd 25: *1sc, sc2tog* (12)

Rnd 26: *sc2tog* (6)

• Close with sl st and finish off, leaving a tail.

LEAVES: Green, make 6

• Ch 11.

• Sl st (3x), *(sl st, ch 2, 3dc in 2nd ch from hook, ch 2, sl st in 2nd ch from hook), sl st* (3x), (ch 2, 3dc in 2nd ch from hook, ch 2, sl st in 2nd ch from hook) in last ch, working in free loops on other side of the chain, *(sl st, ch 2, 3dc in 2nd ch from hook, ch 2, sl st in 2nd ch from hook), sl st* (3x), sl st* (3x) **(see fig. 4c)**

• Finish off, leaving a tail.

• Sew a leaf to each stitch on Rnd 26.

• Weave the finishing tail through the remaining 6sc on Rnd 26 and pull firmly to close the hole. Weave in ends.

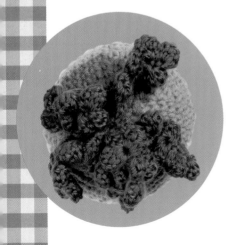

4a

4b

4c

Main Dishes

b.l.t.

BY MELISSA SHEPARD FROM NEW YORK

Bacon is all the rage and this classic sandwich is always a favorite. Designer Melissa Shepard loves to turn little stitches into something that will be loved by all. Well this project is no exception! Get out your frying pan and your crochet hooks because whipping up a B.L.T. has never been so much fun!

what you'll need:

- G/6 crochet hook
- worsted weight yarn in Soft White, Buff, Cherry Red, Tea Leaf, and Claret
- stitch marker
- yarn needle
- embroidery floss
- pair of black safety eyes

FINISHED SIZE: Approx. 4.5" square

Instructions

BREAD: Soft White, make 4
• Ch 18.
Row 1: sc in second ch from hook and in each ch across, ch 1, turn (17) **(see fig. 5a)**
Row 2-20: sc in each sc across, ch 1, turn (17)
Row 21: 5sc in first sc, sc in next 15sc, 5sc in last sc, finish off (25)

EDGING ON BREAD: Buff
• Join with sl st in any sc, sc in each sc and each end of row around with 3sc in each bottom corner of bread. **(see fig. 5b)**
• Sew face onto one slice of bread. Sew on the eyes and use embroidery floss for the smile. Hold 2 slices of bread together and sew together with Buff yarn. Do the same for the other 2 slices. **(see fig. 5c)**

5a

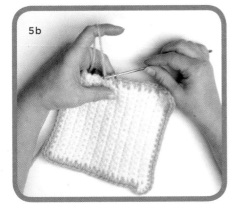

5b

5c

5d

5e

5f

TOMATO: Cherry Red, make 3 or more

• Ch 4, sl st in first ch to form a ring. **(see fig. 5d)**

Rnd 1: ch 1, (sc, ch 1) 10x, sl st in first sc to join (10)

Rnd 2: sl st into next ch 1 space, ch 3, dc into same space as sl st, ch 1, (2dc in next ch 1 space, ch 1) 9x. Join with sl st into top of ch 3 (20) **(see fig. 5e)**

Rnd 3: ch 1, sc in same st as joining and in each dc and each ch around, sl st to join (30) **(see fig. 5f)**

LETTUCE: Tea Leaf, make 2 or more
• Ch 2.
Rnd 1: work 8sc in second ch from hook, join with sl st to first sc (8)
Rnd 2: ch 1, 2sc in same st as joining and in each sc around (16)
Rnd 3: ch 1, sc in same st as joining, 2sc, 1sc, 2sc, (2dc) 8x, (1sc, 2sc) 2x; join with a sl st to first sc (28) **(see fig. 5g)**
Rnd 4: ch 1, sc in same st as joining and in each of the next 7 sts, (2dc, 3dc) 6x, (1sc) 8x; join with sl st to first sc (46) **(see fig. 5h)**
Rnd 5: ch 1, sc in same st as joining and in each of the next 9 sts, (dc) 26x, (sc) 10x, sl st to join (46)

BACON: Claret and Soft White, make 3 or more
• Ch 24 with claret.
Row 1: (1sc) 2x, *sc2tog, (1sc) 2x, 2sc in next st, (1sc) 2x* 3x, ch 1, turn (23)
Row 2: sc in each sc across, changing to soft white on 1, turn (23) **(see fig. 5i)**
Row 3: repeat row 1, changing to claret (23)
Row 4: repeat row 2 (23)
Row 5: repeat row 1, changing to soft white (23)
Row 6: repeat row 2, changing to claret (23)
Row 7: repeat row 1 (23)
Row 8: repeat row 2; finish off

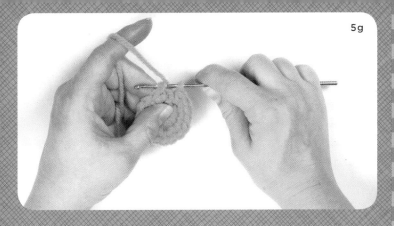

5g

5h

5i

eggs

BY PAMELA DAVIS FROM WASHINGTON

What came first, the chicken or the egg? Either way, after making these, you'll favor the egg. Designed by Seattle-based artist Pamela Davis, aka Mucho Designs, these eggs are going to be a huge hit with all your family and friends. These would make an adorable decoration on your table or in your refrigerator. Yes, you should have adorable crochet things all over your home, even your fridge!

what you'll need:

- C/2 crochet hook
- worsted weight yarn in Yellow and Off-white
- 3 pairs of black safety eyes
- yarn needle
- stuffing

FINISHED SIZE: Approx. 2.5" high

Instructions

WHOLE EGG: Off-white, make 2
• Make adjustable ring.
Row 1: 5sc in ring (5)
Row 2: 2sc in each stitch (10)
Row 3: 2sc in each stitch (20)
Row 4–6: 1sc in each stitch (20)
Row 7: *(1sc) 2x, 2sc in next stitch* until last 2 stitches, (1sc) 2x (26) **(see fig. 6a)**
Row 8-9: 1sc in each stitch (26)
Row 10: *(1sc) 2x, 2sc in next stitch* until last 2 stitches, (1sc) 2x (34)
Row 11–12: 1sc in each stitch (34)
Row 13: *(1sc) 2x, sc2tog* until last 2 stitches, (1sc) 2x (26)
Row 14: *(1sc) 3x, sc2tog* until last stitch, sc in last stitch (21)
Row 15: 1sc in each stitch (21)
Row 16: (1sc) 19x, sc2tog (20)
• Attach safety eyes and sew on smile.
Row 17: (sc2tog) 10x (10)
• Add stuffing.
Row 18: (sc2tog) 5x (5)
• Finish off with sl st and work in tail.

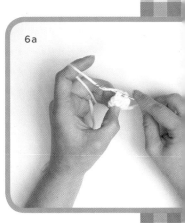

6a

CRACKED EGG TOP: Off-white, make 1
• Make adjustable ring.
Row 1: 5sc in ring (5)
Row 2: 2sc in each st (10) **(see fig. 6b)**
Row 3: 2sc in each st (20)
Row 4: sc in each st (20)
Row 5: (ch 2, sc in 2nd chain from hook, sc in next 2 stitches) 9x, ch 2, sc in 2nd chain from hook, sc in next stitch **(see fig. 6c)**
• Finish off with sl st and work in tail. **(see fig. 6d)**

CRACKED EGG BOTTOM: Off-white, make 1
• Make adjustable ring.
Row 1: 5sc in ring (5)
Row 2: 2sc in each stitch (10)
Row 3: *1sc in next st, 2sc in next 1st (15)
Row 4: *1sc in next st, 2sc in next 1st, 1sc (22)
Row 5-6: 1sc in each st (22)
Row 7: *(1sc) 2x, 1sc in next stitch* until last stitch, 2sc in last st (30)
Row 8-10: 1sc in each stitch (30)
Row 11: *(1sc) 2x, skip 1 st* (20)
Row 12: (1sc chain 2, sc in 2nd chain from hook, sc in next stitch) 10x
• Finish off with sl st and work in tail.

CRACKED EGG YOLK: Yellow, make 1
• Make adjustable ring.
Row 1: 6sc in ring (6)
Row 2: 2sc in each stitch (12)
Row 3: 2sc in each stitch (24)
Row 4-5: 1sc in each stitch (24)
Row 6: *1sc in next 2 stitches, 2sc in next stitch* (32)
Row 7-8: 1sc in each stitch (32)
Row 9: *1sc in next 2 stitches, sc2tog* (24)
• Attach safety eyes and sew on mouth.
Row 10: (sc2tog) 12x (12)
• Add stuffing.
Row 11: (sc2tog) 6x (6)
• Close with sl st, work
  in tail.

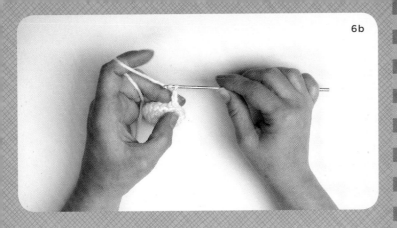

6b

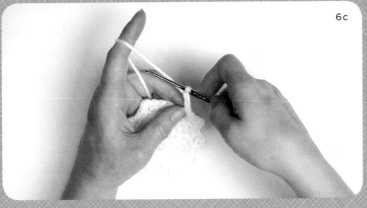

6c

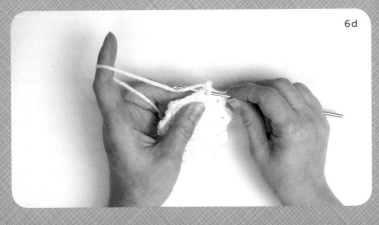

6d

project
7

hamburger

BY ALICIA KACHMAR FROM PENNSYLVANIA

Another great project by Alicia Kachmar of Eternal Sunshine fame, this hamburger is both good for your carnivore and vegan friends! You can add your favorite condiments to make this all your own. Great project to make for kids who love to play with their food! The best part? No animals were hurt creating this delicious burger.

what you'll need:

- F/5 crochet hook
- worsted weight yarn in Tan, Off-white, Chocolate Brown, Fire Engine Red, Golden Yellow, Grass Green, and Purple
- pair of black safety eyes
- black embroidery thread
- yarn needle
- stuffing

FINISHED SIZE: Approx. 6" tall

Instructions

HAMBURGER PATTY: Chocolate Brown, make 2
• Make adjustable ring.
Rnd 1: 7sc in ring (7)
Rnd 2: 2sc in each stitch (14)
Rnd 3: *1sc, 2sc in next st* (21)
Rnd 4: *(1sc) 2x, 2sc in next st* (28)
Rnd 5: *(1sc) 3x, 2sc in next st* (35)
Rnd 6: *(1sc) 4x, 2sc in next st* (42)
Rnd 7: *(1sc) 5x, 2sc in next st* (49)
Rnd 8: 1sc in each stitch (49)
Rnd 9: *(1sc) 6x, 2sc in next st* (56)
Rnd 10: 1sc in each stitch (56)
• Close with a sl st, leaving a long tail
  for sewing on one of the pieces.
• Sew both pieces together with the
  wrong sides facing out, and stuff.
  (see fig. 7a)

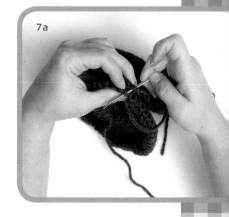

7a

HAMBURGER BUN, BOTTOM: Tan
• Make adjustable ring.
Rnd 1: 9sc in ring (9)
Rnd 2: 2sc in each stitch (18)
Rnd 3: *1sc, 2sc in next st* (27)
Rnd 4: *(1sc) 2x, 2sc in next st* (36)
Rnd 5: *(1sc) 3x, 2sc in next st* (45)
Rnd 6: *(1sc) 4x, 2sc in next st* (54)
Rnd 7: 1sc in each stitch (54)
Rnd 8: *sc2tog, (1sc) 7x* (48)
Rnd 9: 1sc in each stitch (48)
• Close with a sl st.

7b

7c

7d

HAMBURGER BUN, TOP: Tan

• Make adjustable ring.

Rnd 1: 9sc in ring (9)

Rnd 2: 2sc in each stitch (18)

Rnd 3: *1sc, 2sc in next st* (27)

Rnd 4: *(1sc) 2x, 2sc in next st* (36)

Rnd 5: *(1sc) 3x, 2sc in next st* (45)

Rnd 6: *(1sc) 4x, 2sc in next st* (54)

Rnd 7: *(1sc) 5x, 2sc in next st* (63)

Rnds 8–9: 1sc in each stitch (63)

Rnd 10: *sc2tog, (1sc) 4x* (56)

Rnd 11: *sc2tog, (1sc) 6x* (49)

• Close with a sl st.

• With off-white yarn, make "sesame seeds" by making 5-mm stitches all over the top bun, as shown in picture. **(see fig. 7b)**

• Attach safety eyes and sew on mouth.

HAMBURGER BUN, INTERIOR: Off-white, make 2

• Make adjustable ring.

Rnd 1: 9sc in ring (9)

Rnd 2: 2sc in each stitch (18)

Rnd 3: *1sc, 2sc in next st* (27)

Rnd 4: *(1sc) 2x, 2sc in next st* (36)

Rnd 5: *(1sc) 3x, 2sc in next st* (45)

Rnd 6: *(1sc) 4x, 2sc in next st* (54)

(see fig. 7c)

Rnd 7: *(1sc) 5x, 2sc in next st* (63)

Rnd 8: 1sc in each stitch (63)

• Close with a sl st and leave a long tail for sewing.

• With the hamburger bun top and one of the bun insides, stuffing as you go along, sew together with the wrong sides facing out. Repeat with hamburger bun bottom and other bun inside. **(see fig. 7d)**

CHEESE SLICE: Golden Yellow
• Ch 15
Rnds 1–13: 1sc in each stitch, ch 1, turn
Rnd 14: 1sc in each stitch, ch 1
• 3sc in corner, sc into each row down the side, 3sc in corner, sc across into each sc across bottom, 3sc in corner, sc into each row up the side, 3sc in corner. (see fig. 7e)
• Close with a sl st.

LETTUCE: Grass Green
• Make adjustable ring.
Rnd 1: 6sc in ring (6)
Rnd 2: 2sc in each stitch (12)
Rnd 3: *1sc, 2sc in next st* (18) (see fig. 7f)
Rnd 4: *(1sc) 2x, 2sc in next st* (24)
Rnd 5: *(1sc) 3x, 2sc in next st* (30)
Rnd 6: *(1sc) 4x, 2sc in next st* (36)
Rnd 7: *(1sc) 5x, 2sc in next st* (42)
Rnd 8: 2sc in each stitch around (84)
Rnd 9: ch 3, 2dc, dc, dc; *2dc, dc, dc, dc* (106)
• Close with a sl st.

TOMATO SLICE: Fire Engine Red
• Make adjustable ring.
Rnd 1: 6sc in ring (6)
Rnd 2: 2sc in each stitch and join (12)
Rnd 3: *ch 5, skip 1 stitch, 1sc in next* 6x
Rnd 4: ch 3, *4dc in 5 ch space, dc in sc* 6x
• Close with a sl st in the 3rd ch of first ch 3 of previous round.

ONION: Off-white and Purple, make 2
• With white yarn, ch 34 and join to first ch. Join with purple yarn, cutting white. Sl st with purple around. (see fig. 7g)
• Close with a sl st.

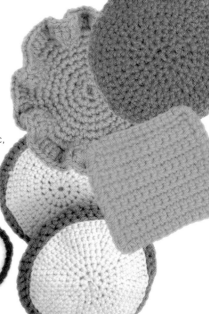

7e

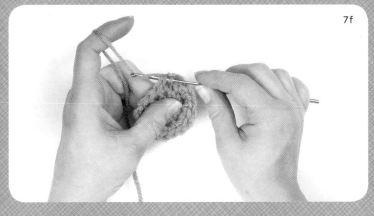

7f

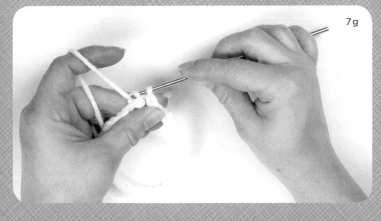

7g

hot dog

BY ALICIA KACHMAR FROM PENNSYLVANIA

- -

Hot diggity dog! This plump little dog would be great on the grill, but no flames please! The best part about this little weiner is that he's appetizing to both your carnivore and vegetarian friends! Designed by Alicia Kachmar, you can easily create a whole feast as party favors for your next barbeque.

what you'll need:

- F/5 crochet hook
- worsted weight yarn in Tan, Off-white, Burnt Orange, Cherry Red, and Bright Yellow
- pair of black safety eyes
- black embroidery thread
- yarn needle
- stuffing

FINISHED SIZE: Approx. 6" long

Instructions

HOT DOG: Burnt Orange
• Make adjustable ring.
Rnd 1: 6sc in ring (6)
Rnd 2: *1sc, 2sc in next stitch* (9)
Rnd 3: 2sc, (1sc) 2x, 2sc, (1sc) 5x (11)
Rnds 4–18: 1sc in each stitch (11)
Rnd 19: sc2tog, (1sc) 2x, sc2tog, (1sc) 5x (9)
• Add stuffing.
• Sew on eyes and embroider on mouth.
Rnd 20: sc2tog, (1sc) 2x, sc2tog, sc, sc2tog (6)
• Skip 2sc and sl st to next stitch.

KETCHUP AND MUSTARD TOPPINGS:
Cherry Red and Bright Yellow
• With red yarn, ch 20, leaving a
   long tail for sewing.
• With yellow yarn, ch 20, leaving
   a long tail for sewing.
• Sew squiggles onto hot dog,
   beginning below the mouth and
   angling down the hot dog as
   you sew **(see fig. 8a)**

8a

OUTSIDE OF BUN: Tan, make 2
• Ch 20 with tan.
Rnd 1: (1sc) 19x; 2sc in the last
stitch; 1sc in each free loop until
the last loop; 2sc in the last free
loop (40) **(see fig. 8b)**
Rnd 2: (2sc) 2x, (1sc) 18x, (2sc) 2x,
(1sc) 18x (44)
Rnd 3: (2sc) 4x, (1sc) 20x, (2sc)
4x, (1sc) 20x (52)
• Close with a sl st, leaving a long
   tail on one piece only.

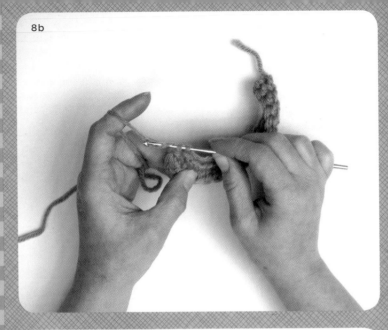

INSIDE OF BUN: Off-white, make 2
• Ch 19.
Rnd 1: 1sc in each stitch until the last stitch; 2sc in the last stitch; 1sc in each free loop until the last loop; 2sc in the last free loop (38)
Rnd 2: (2sc) 2x, (1sc) 17x, (2sc) 2x, (1sc) 17x (42)
Rnds 3–4: 1sc in each stitch (42)
• Close with sl st, leaving a long tail for sewing.

TO ASSEMBLE:
• With wrong side on the outside, stuff tan pieces with stuffing.
• With tail of off-white piece, sew into the inner loops of the last round of each tan piece. **(see fig. 8c)**
• With tail of tan piece, sew two pieces of bun together by sewing into 18 stitches where the pieces meet.

sushi rolls

BY ELISHA COPELAND FROM TEXAS

Even if you're not a master of rolling sushi, you can whip up some of these little guys in no time! This pattern can be modified to create a whole variety of flavors by simply changing yarn colors or adding felt to create wasabi, ginger, or small veggies on top. Chopsticks not required!

what you'll need:

- G/6 crochet hook
- worsted weight yarn in White, Black, Multicolor Green, and Multicolor Red
- stitch marker
- 4 pairs of black safety eyes
- black embroidery thread
- stuffing
- scissors

FINISHED SIZE: Approx. 1.5" tall and 2" around

Instructions

SUSHI AVOCADO OR SALMON ROLL:
Make 2 each
• Worked in continuous rounds.
• Ch 2 (in the multi green or multi red). **(see fig. 9a)**
Rnd 1: sc6 in second chain to form a ring
Rnd 2: 2sc in each stitch (12), then start your stitch marker
• Cut yarn, leaving a 3" tail.
Rnd 3: using white yarn, *2sc, 1sc* repeat around to stitch marker (18)
Rnd 4: *(1sc) 2x, 2sc* repeat around to stitch marker (24)
• Cut yarn, leaving a 3" tail.
Rnd 5: using black yarn, sc around in the back loops only to end of round **(see fig. 9b)**
Rnd 6-9: (1sc) 24x
• Cut black, leaving a 3" tail, and join in white.
Rnd 10: sc in this round in back loops only **(see fig. 9c)**
Rnd 11: decrease around until complete (approx. 2" around) stuffing as you go **(see figs. 9d and 9e)**
• Attach safety eyes and sew on mouths.

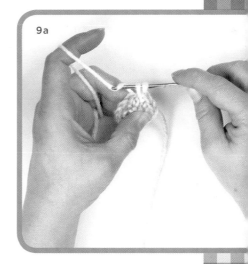

9a

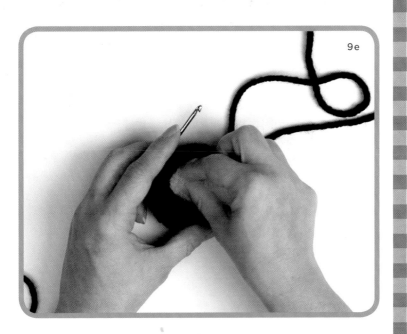

9e

Desserts

cupcakes

BY HOLLY COLEMAN FROM HAWAII

These cupcakes really do take the cake. Sure to make any party complete, you can start with these as your basics and work from there to create your own! Designed by Holly Coleman, it's easy to mix and match colors and toppings.

what you'll need:

- C/2 crochet hook
- worsted weight yarn
- stuffing
- 3 pairs of black safety eyes
- yarn needle
- scissors
- embroidery needle
- embroidery thread

FINISHED SIZE: Approx. 4.5" high

Instructions

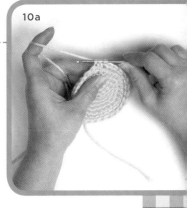

10a

VARIATIONS

MINT CUPCAKE: Light Brown bottom, Mint Green frosting, White whipped cream puff, and Pink berry

VANILLA CUPCAKE: Light Brown bottom, Lemon frosting, Brown glaze, White whipped cream puff, Red berry

CHOCOLATE CUPCAKE: Light Pink bottom, Dark Brown frosting, White and Dark Brown glaze, Light Pink berry

CUPCAKE BOTTOM:

• Make adjustable ring.

Rnd 1: 6sc in ring (6)

Rnd 2: 2sc in each stitch (12)

Rnd 3: *1sc, 2sc in next st* (18)

Rnd 4: *(1sc) 2x, 2sc in next st* (24)

Rnd 5: *(1sc) 3x, 2sc in next st* (30)

Rnd 6: *(1sc) 4x, 2sc in next st* (36)

Rnd 7: *(1sc) 4x, sc2tog* in back loops only (30) **(see fig. 10a)**

Rnd 8: *(1sc) 4x, 2sc in next st* (36)

Rnd 9: 1sc in each stitch (36)

Rnd 10: *(1sc) 5x, 2sc in next st* (42)

Rnd 11–16: 1sc in each stitch (42)

• Close with sl st, leaving tail for sewing.

• Attach safety eyes and sew on mouth. **(see fig. 10b)**

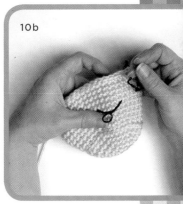

10b

FROSTING:

• Make adjustable ring.

Rnd 1: 6sc in ring (6)

Rnd 2: 2sc in each stitch (12)

Rnd 3: *1sc, 2sc in next st* (18)

Rnd 4: *(1sc) 2x, 2sc in next st* (24)

Rnd 5: *(1sc) 3x, 2sc in next st* (30)

Rnd 6: *(1sc) 4x, 2sc in next st* (36)

10c

10d

10e

Rnd 7: *(1sc) 5x, 2sc in next st* (42)

Rnd 8-9: 1sc in each stitch (42)

Rnd 10: *5dc in next stitch, skip next stitch, sl st* (84) **(see fig. 10c)**

• End with sl st, leaving tail for sewing.

GLAZE:

• Make adjustable ring.

Rnd 1: 6sc in ring (6)

Rnd 2: 3dc in each stitch (18)

Rnd 3: 2dc in each stitch (36)

Rnd 4: *(1sl st) 2x, 1 hdc in next st, 2dc in each of the next 2 st* (42)

• Close with sl st, leaving tail for sewing.

SWIRL:

• In the spaces between rows, and starting in the center of the glaze, pull a loop of new yarn with your hook from the underside to the topside. **(see figs. 10d and 10e)**

• Repeat to draw another loop into and through the first.

• Repeat 52 times or until swirl reaches the end of the glaze.

WHIPPED CREAM PUFF: make 2, sew together in the middle

• Make adjustable ring.

Rnd 1: 6sc in ring (6)

Rnd 2: 5dc in each stitch (30)

BERRY:

• Make adjustable ring.

Rnd 1: 6sc in ring (6)

Rnd 2: 2sc in each stitch (12)

Rnd 3-5: 1sc in each stitch (12)

• Add stuffing.

Rnd 6: (sc2tog) 6x (6)

• Close with sl st, leaving tail for sewing.

donuts

BY DENISE FERGUSON FROM PENNSYLVANIA

Whether you're in the mood for breakfast or dessert, these colorful donuts made by Denise Ferguson of Yummy Pancake are always appropriate. This project is so much fun because you can easily make a whole dozen with different color variations and sprinkle options! The best part? No sticky fingers!

what you'll need:

- C/2 crochet hook
- worsted weight yarn
- 3 pairs of black safety eyes
- yarn needle
- stuffing

FINISHED SIZE: Approx. 4.5" wide

Instructions

11a

VARIATIONS
CHOCOLATE DONUT WITH WHITE FROSTING: Chocolate Brown donut, Bright White frosting, Jet Black mouth, Candy Pink sprinkles
WHITE WITH PINK FROSTING: Bright White donut, Candy Pink frosting, Jet Black mouth, Red sprinkles
PLAIN WITH CHOCOLATE FROSTING: Bone Brown donut, Chocolate Brown frosting, Candy Pink mouth

DONUT:
• Chain 24, join to form a ring.
Rnd 1: 1sc in each st (24)
Rnd 2: *1sc, 2sc in next st* (36) **(see fig. 11a)**
Rnd 3: 1sc in each st (36)
Rnd 4: *1sc, 2sc in next st* (54)
Rnd 5–12: 1sc in each st (54)
Rnd 13: *1sc, sc2tog* (36)
Rnd 14: 1sc in each st (36)
Rnd 15: *1sc, sc2tog* (24)
Rnd 16: 1sc in each st (24)
• Sew Round 1 and Round 16 together, stuffing as you sew. Sew on frosting. **(see figs. 11b and 11c)**

FROSTING:
• With each color: chain 24, join to form a ring.
Rnd 1: 1sc in each st (24)
Rnd 2: *1sc, 2sc in next st* (36)
Rnd 3: 1sc in each st (36)
Rnd 4: *1sc, 2sc in next st* (54)
Rnd 5–7: 1sc in each st (54)

Rnd 8: *4sc in next st, skip next st, 1sc*
• Attach eyes, and sew on mouth and sprinkles.

TO ASSEMBLE:
• Using a yarn needle, sew the frosting piece around the inside edge and outside edge securely to the donut. **(see figs. 11d and 11e)**

11b

11c

11d

11e

tea & cookies

BY DENISE FERGUSON FROM PENNSYLVANIA

When it's time to unwind from a long day, a warm cup of tea and a few delicious cookies are just the treat. Cute, delicious, and fun to make, this project is especially satisfying because you can style the cookies to your liking. These adorable patterns made by Denise Ferguson of Yummy Pancake are a perfect cozy afternoon project!

what you'll need:

- C/2 crochet hook
- worsted weight yarn in Tan, Bright White, Royal Blue, and Jet Black (Tea Cup); Tan, Cocoa Brown, and Jet Black (Chocolate Chip Cookie); Tan, Bright White, Chocolate Brown, and Jet Black (Black and White Cookie)
- 3 pairs of black safety eyes
- yarn needle
- stuffing

FINISHED SIZE: CUP: Approx. 3.5″ wide; COOKIES: Approx. 3″ wide

Instructions

TEACUP:

TOP OF TEACUP: Tan
• Make adjustable ring.
Rnd 1: 6sc in ring (6)
Rnd 2: 2sc in each stitch (12)
Rnd 3: *1sc, 2sc in next stitch* (18)
Rnd 4: *(1sc) 2x, 2sc in next st* (24)
Rnd 5: *(1sc) 3x, 2sc in next st* (30)
Rnd 6: *(1sc) 4x, 2sc in next st* (36)
Rnd 7: *(1sc) 5x, 2sc in next st* (42)
Rnd 8: *(1sc) 6x, 2sc in next st* (48)
• Finish off.

HANDLE: Bright White
• Make adjustable ring.
Rnd 1: 6sc in ring (6)
Rnd 2–11: 1sc in each st (6)
• Finish off.

TEACUP BOTTOM: Bright White and
Royal Blue
• Make adjustable ring.
Rnd 1: 6sc in ring (6)
Rnd 2: 2sc in each stitch (12)
Rnd 3: *1sc, 2sc in next
stitch* (18)
Rnd 4: *(1sc) 2x, 2sc in next
st* (24)
Rnd 5: in back stitch only,
1sc around (24)
Rnd 6: *(1sc) 3x, 2sc in next
st* (30)

Rnd 7: *(1sc) 4x, 2sc in next st* (36)
Rnd 8: *(1sc) 5x, 2sc in next st* (42)
Rnd 9: *(1sc) 6x, 2sc in next st* (48)
Rnd 10–14: 1sc in each st (48)
Rnd 15: with blue yarn, 1sc in each st (48)
• Finish off. Add eyes and sew on mouth. Sew on handle.
• To complete the teacup, you will crochet through both the teacup bottom and top.
Rnd 16: with white yarn, 1sc in each st (through both the teacup top and bottom), stuffing as you go (48)
• Finish off.

TO ASSEMBLE:
• Take the piece you crocheted for the handle and sew the top and bottom to the side of the teacup with a yarn needle to create the cup handle. **(see fig. 12a)**

COOKIE: Tan, make 2
• Make adjustable ring.
Rnd 1: 6sc in ring (6)
Rnd 2: 2sc in each stitch (12)
(see figs. 12b and 12c)
Rnd 3: *1sc, 2sc in next st* (18)
Rnd 4: *1sc, 2sc in next st* (27)
Rnd 5: 1sc in each stitch (27)
Rnd 6: *1sc, 2sc in next st* (40)
Rnd 7: 1sc in each stitch (40)

CHOCOLATE CHIP COOKIE:
Follow the Cookie pattern. Add eyes, embroider on mouth, and add chocolate chips using French knots in Cocoa Brown on one side of cookie. **(see figs. 12d and 12e)** Sew both sides of cookie together and stuff as you go. **(see figs. 12f and 12g)**

BLACK AND WHITE COOKIE:
Bright White and Chocolate Brown
• Make adjustable ring.
Row 1: 3sc in ring, ch 1, turn (3)
Row 2: 2sc in each st, ch 1, turn (6)
Row 3: *1sc, 2sc in next st* ch 1, turn (9)
Row 4: *1sc, 2sc in next st* ch 1, turn (13)
Row 5: *1sc, 2sc in next st* ch 1, (19)
• Sew each frosting color half on one cookie side. **(see fig. 12h)**
• Add eyes and embroider on mouth. Sew both sides of cookie together and stuff as you go.

12a

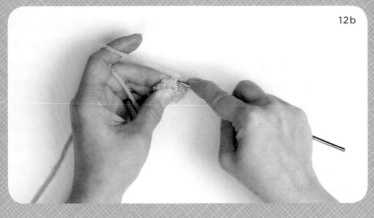

12b

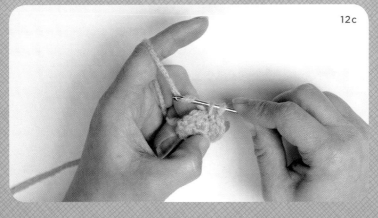

12c

12d

12e

12f

12g

12h

About the Author

Kristen Rask owns the urban toy boutique Schmancy in downtown Seattle, where she sells her own handmade goods and items from other artists. She attributes her love for the craft marketplace to selling friendship bracelets at summer camp during her childhood, and her passion hasn't dwindled since. Kristen is the author of the *Creature Crochet* kit (2009), and the books *Plush You! Lovable Misfits to Sew and Stuff* (2007) and *Button and Stitch: Supercute Ways to Use Your Button Stash* (2010).

Acknowledgments

I would like to give a huge thanks to all of the wonderful artists who contributed to this kit. Without you, it wouldn't have been possible.

To Amelia Riedler for being a pure pleasure to work with and being so patient.

To my family and friends, your endless support is not taken lightly.

Lastly, to the Plush You! supporters, without which none of this would have happened to me.

Where to Find the Artists

Tristine Benedict finds most of her inspiration from cookbooks and bakeries. This mom of two gets a stamp of approval for all her patterns from her kids and then puts them on her online shop.
www.stayhomecupcake.etsy.com.

Holly Coleman clearly knows how to create kawaii lovables! You will be swooning in no time!
www.berrysprite.etsy.com.

Elisha Copeland has a shop that makes you feel like you walked into the best candy shop ever. Everything is colorful and cute.
www.elishacopeland.etsy.com.

Pamela Davis is a woman of many talents, including crochet and embroidery floss.
www.muchodesign.etsy.com.

Denise Ferguson of Yummy Pancake fame has captured the hearts of many amigurumi lovers by turning your favorite foods and appliances into adorable squishy friends.
www.yummypancake.com.

Alicia Kachmar has a lot under her belt. Her book *Witch Craft* came out in 2010, and she always has some new crafting up her sleeve.
www.aliciakachmar.com.

Anna Moscioni has sold thousands of patterns on Etsy, from sweet treats to cute animals. Anna crochets it all!
www.craftyanna.etsy.com.

Melissa Shepard makes all kinds of crocheted items. From cute to practical, she can make anything both kids and adults can appreciate.
www.honeybee69.etsy.com.

STERLING INNOVATION
New York

An Imprint of Sterling Publishing
387 Park Avenue South
New York, NY 10016

STERLING INNOVATION and the distinctive Sterling Innovation logo
are registered trademarks of Sterling Publishing Co., Inc.

© 2011 by becker&mayer! LLC

This 2011 edition published by Sterling Publishing Co., Inc. by arrangement with
becker&mayer! Books, Bellevue, Washington.
www.beckermayer.com

All rights reserved. No part of this publication may be reproduced, stored
in a retrieval system, or transmitted, in any form or by any means, electronic,
mechanical, photocopying, recording, or otherwise, without prior
written permission from the publisher.

Design: Jamison Spittler
Editorial: Amelia Riedler
Production Coordination: Shirley Woo
Product Development: Lauren Cavanaugh and Peter Schumacher

ISBN 978-1-4351-3291-7

This book is part of the *Yummy Crochet* kit and is not to be sold separately.

For information about custom editions, special sales, and premium and corporate
purchases, please contact Sterling Special Sales at 800-805-5489 or
specialsales@sterlingpublishing.com.

Printed, manufactured, and assembled by
Starlite Development Limited, Shenzhen, China

2 4 6 8 10 9 7 5 3

www.sterlingpublishing.com

Project #11122